Soup Maker Recipe Book

100 Delicious & Nutritious
Soup Recipes
By

Liana Green

I blog at:

www.LianasKitchen.co.uk

My Amazon Author Page:

www.amazon.co.uk/Liana-Green

www.amazon.com/Liana-Green

Copyright ©2016 by Liana Green

All rights reserved. This book or any portion thereof may not be reproduced or used in any manner whatsoever without the express written permission of the publisher except for the use of brief quotations in a book review.

DISCLAIMER

This book is not intended as a substitute for the medical advice of doctors/physicians. The reader should regularly consult a physician/doctor in matters relating to his/her health and particularly with respect to any symptoms that may require diagnosis or medical attention. Although the author and publisher have made every effort to ensure that the information in this book was correct at press time, the author and publisher do not assume and hereby disclaim any liability to any part for any loss, damage, or disruption caused by errors or omissions, whether such errors or omissions result from negligence, accident or any other cause.

Homemade Soup

Soups can be anything you want them to be. Something light for lunch, served as a starter, or something more substantial for dinner. Sometimes I even have one as a mid-afternoon pick me up.

They are nutritious, filling, and easy to incorporate in your daily diet. They can be low calorie – useful if you are on a calorie controlled eating plan. They ensure you get all the nutrients you need.

Choose from traditional soups, such as Butternut Squash or Leek and Potato, or experiment with more unique soup recipes like Curried Banana or Beetroot and Apple. They all taste delicious.

Try making a large batch and freezing the individual portions, defrosting them when you need them.

Soups aren't just for the colder months (although they do a brilliant job of making you feel snuggled and warm); you can enjoy soup year round.

They are an economical method of cooking too. Use up those stray ingredients in the fridge and leftover meats from Sunday Roasts.

The Basics of Soup Making

Soups can be made with minimal kitchen equipment (a saucepan, stove and blender), or with the help of a soup maker or slow cooker.

Although this soup maker recipe book is aimed towards making soup with a soup maker (in particular a Morphy Richards Soup Maker) the recipes can easily be adapted to using a saucepan and stove.

Stock

For the most delicious tasting soup use, homemade stock. Not only does it really enhance the taste of your soup, it is also better for you than stock cubes.

If you make a batch of it you can keep it in the fridge for up to 3 days, or freeze portions in the freezer for up to 3 months.

For stock recipes and some tips on making it, see the last chapter in the book 'Homemade Stock Recipes.'

Of course it isn't always feasible to make your own homemade stock, and if you can't, don't let it stop you from making and enjoying soup. I probably use my own stock half of the time, versus stock cubes/fresh stock found in the chilled section of the supermarket. Always look at the salt content (and any other ingredients) before buying premade stock, and try to go for the low sodium varieties.

If I am using stock cubes or bouillon powder I will only use 1 cube per recipe. So, if the recipe asks for 850ml vegetable stock I will put one stock cube in 850ml of boiling water.

Do I Need To Sauté?

Some soup makers come with a built in sauté feature. The model I own has one and it is very useful. If yours doesn't it is still simple enough to sauté ingredients in a pan on the stove and just transfer them over to the soup maker when they are done.

Sautéing certain ingredients help to draw out their flavours that simply cooking in the stock won't. Onions would usually go in first to allow them to caramelise, followed by other vegetables (like carrots and celery), and with crushed or minced garlic added last in the sauté step as it takes the least amount of time to cook.

If you are in a rush you can skip the sauté step and your soup will still taste great, but the sautéing does add a more flavoursome result.

Should I Add Salt?

This is a matter of personal and dietary preferences. I rarely add salt to my soup, but if I do, it is only at the end once I have tasted the soup.

Also, if you are using stock cubes, consider the salt content – if need be go for a reduced salt brand. Tinned tomatoes and pastes can also contain more salt than you think.

It is for this reason that I haven't added any salt in the ingredients – but of course add some if you prefer.

How Long Will My Soup Last?

In our house, not very long! (But we are a family of five). On the occasions that we don't all have the soup I have made, I will keep any leftovers in the fridge for up to 3 days, or divide into portions and keep in the freezer for up to 3 months. I simply defrost and reheat when I want to have them. Just make sure you allow the soup to cool sufficiently before putting in the fridge of freezer.

How Can I Make My Soup Creamier?

Some of the recipes in this book are already creamy versions – but what if you want to turn some of the other recipes into creamy, thicker versions too?

The obvious answer is of course to add cream – but wait until the soup has finished cooking and then stir in some cream, a tablespoon at a time until you get to your desired thickness. You can use double cream, single cream, crème fraiche, yoghurt, milk or even coconut milk for a dairy free alternative. You can also use breadcrumbs; just stir them in a few minutes before the end of the soup cooking time.

Garnishes and Soup Boosters

Garnishes are optional on soups but can add a nice extra taste, as well as make them visually more appealing. Try chopped herbs such as chives, parsley, coriander or basil.

A swirl of cream, grated cheese or the zest of a lemon or lime also works well.

Croutons also make a nice addition – either buy some from the supermarket or make your own. You will find a recipe for croutons after the homemade stock recipes at the end of the book.

You can boost your soup further by sprinkling on seeds or nuts, including sunflower, pumpkin, sesame or chopped almonds, Brazil nuts and cashew, among others.

Using a Soup Maker

If you don't already have a soup maker and you are considering getting one, you need to think about the different types available.

I have a Morphy Richards Soup Maker. I ended up getting the Sauté version because I wanted to be able to make everything in it without having to use a saucepan. It also didn't cost much more than the model without the sauté feature. If you want to take a look at my research and review on the different soup makers you can check them out on my blog:

www.lianaskitchen.co.uk/soup-makers

Using This Book

The recipes in this book have been created and tested using the Morphy Richards soup maker. But that absolutely doesn't mean you can't make them in a different soup maker model. Just double check your manufacturer's instructions – especially concerning the maximum and minimum levels of liquid and ingredients they can hold.

Servings

Each of my recipes suggests a serving size of 4. However, they are 4 large portions and could easily be stretched to 6, especially if you are having them as a starter or snack.

Calories

I have calculated the calories for each recipe. They may of course vary depending on the exact brand or quantity of ingredient you use. The calorie amount should give you a rough idea though.

Measurements

I have used metric measurements when writing out my recipes. I have however provided a conversion table should you wish to convert them.

I have listed the measurements that I used with each recipe - but you may need to adjust some depending on what ingredients you are using, and what soup maker you have. But that is the beauty of soup making; you can adjust quantities and usually get the same tasty results!

The measurement I find that varies the most are the stock volumes. Sometimes I need to put more in and sometimes less. Just always make sure your levels sit within the minimum and maximum recommendations.

If you want to make a thinner soup add more liquid, and conversely, if you prefer it thicker, reduce the liquid levels.

Most of all have fun making soup. Experiment with these recipes, use them as they are or use them as a guide. Change ingredients around and add some in. You can't really go that wrong!

Conversion Table

VOLUME

ML	FL OZ	CUP
250	8	1
180	6	3/4
150	5	2/3
120	4	1/2
75	2 ½	1/3
60	2	1/4
30	1	1/8
15	½	1 tablespoon

WEIGHT

G	OZ
15	1\2
30	1
60	2
90	3
110	4
140	5
170	6
200	7
225	8
255	9

VEGETABLE SOUPS

Roast Tomato & Chili

Serves 4   Calories: 122 (per serving)

Ingredients

2tbsp olive oil

1 medium onion, chopped

3 garlic cloves, crushed

500g ripe tomatoes, sliced in half

2 red chilies, sliced (deseed if you prefer a milder taste)

900ml vegetable stock

Making It

In a preheated oven (190C/Gas Mark 5) lay the tomato halves on a baking tray and drizzle with 1tbsp of the olive oil. Roast for around 25 minutes or until the tomatoes have softened.

Heat the remaining oil in the soup maker jug if it has a sauté function. If not, heat the oil in a saucepan.

Add the chopped onion and sauté for 3 to 4 minutes, stirring occasionally. Add the crushed garlic and sliced chilies. Sauté for a further 1 or 2 minutes.

Switch off the sauté function/transfer ingredients to your soup maker.

Add the tomatoes and vegetable stock, taking care to stay between the MAX and MIN lines on your soup maker. Top up with more boiling water if required.

Set the soup maker off on the smooth setting.

Butternut Squash

Ingredients

2 tbsp. olive oil

500g butternut squash, diced

1 medium onion, chopped

5 cloves garlic, crushed

1tsp ground cumin

1 red chilli finely sliced (seeds optional)

1tsp fresh root ginger, grated

800ml vegetable stock

200ml coconut milk light

1 Juice of lime

Making It

Heat oil in soup maker jug if it has a sauté function. If not, heat the oil in a saucepan.

Add the diced butternut squash and sauté for 3 to 4 minutes, stirring occasionally.

Add the red chilli, ground cumin, onion and continue to sauté for a further 5 minutes or until the ingredients start to soften. Continue to stir during this time.

Switch off the sauté function/transfer ingredients to your soup maker.

Add the rest of the ingredients and stir to evenly distribute.

Put the lid on the jug and press the chunky setting.

Honey Roast Parsnip

Serves 4   Calories 163 (per serving)

Ingredients

1tbsp. olive oil

1 medium onion, chopped

3 large spring onions, chopped

400g parsnips (approx. 5), peeled and chopped

2 tbsp. honey

1tsp mixed dried herbs

900ml vegetable stock

Making It

Preheat the oven to 190C/Gas Mark 5

Mix the honey and oil together in a bowl. Lay the chopped parsnips out in a baking tray. Brush the honey and oil across them all, ensuring they are all coated. Sprinkle the mixed dried herbs over them.

Put in the oven and roast for about 30 minutes, or until the parsnips are soft.

Remove from the oven and add to your soup maker, together with the remaining ingredients. Stir to combine.

Ensure you don't go above the MAX line in your soup maker. If needed, top up to the MIN line with hot water.

Put the lid on and select the smooth setting.

Sweet Potato and Leek

Serves 4   Calories: 164 (per serving)

Ingredients

1 tbsp. olive oil

1 medium onion, chopped

2 garlic cloves, crushed

3 medium leeks (approx. 300g), chopped

2 sweet potatoes (approx. 300g), peeled and chopped

800ml vegetable stock

1 tbsp. fresh parsley, chopped (optional for garnish)

Making It

Heat the olive oil in your soup maker if it has a sauté function, if not, heat it in a saucepan.

Add the onion and garlic and sauté for about 3-5 minutes.

Switch off the sauté function on your soup maker/transfer from saucepan to soup maker.

Add remaining ingredients, apart from the parsley. Stir to combine well.

Ensure you don't go above the MAX line in your soup maker. If needed, top up to the MIN line with hot water.

Put the lid on and select the smooth setting.

Garnish with chopped parsley (optional).

Chilli Bean

Serves 4   Calories: 198 (per serving)

Ingredients

1tbsp olive oil

1 medium onion, chopped

1 medium carrot, chopped

400g can of kidney beans, drained

400g can of chopped tomatoes

1tbsp tomato puree

1tsp mild chilli powder

750ml vegetable stock

Making It

Heat the olive oil in your soup maker if it has a sauté function, if not, heat it in a saucepan.

Add the onion and sauté for about 3-5 minutes.

Add the chopped carrot and sauté for a further 2 minutes.

Add the kidney beans and chilli powder and sauté for a further 1 minute.

Switch off the sauté function on your soup maker/transfer from saucepan to soup maker.

Add remaining ingredients. Stir to combine well.

Ensure you don't go above the MAX line in your soup maker. If needed, top up to the MIN line with hot water.

Put the lid on and select the chunky setting.

Garnish with chopped parsley (optional).

New Potato and Mint

Serves 4   Calories: 93 (per serving)

Ingredients

1 tbsp. olive oil

1 medium onion, chopped

2 garlic cloves, crushed

250g new potatoes, chopped in half

10g fresh mint

2 tbsp. single cream

800ml vegetable stock

Chives for garnish (optional)

Making It

Heat the olive oil in your saucepan or in your soup maker if it has a sauté function.

Add the chopped onion and sauté for 2 to 3 minutes.

Add the crushed garlic and sauté for a further minute.

Switch off the sauté function/transfer ingredients from saucepan to your soup maker.

Add the remaining ingredients apart from the cream.

Set on smooth setting.

Once finished, add the cream and use the blend function to mix.

Garnish with a few chopped up chives and season with salt and pepper if required.

Moroccan Chickpea Soup

Serves 4   Calories: 129 (per serving)

Ingredients

1 tbsp. olive oil

1 celery stalk, chopped finely

1 small carrot, peeled and chopped finely

1 medium onion, chopped finely

2 garlic cloves, crushed

400g can chickpea, rinsed and drained

400g can chopped tomatoes

½ tsp. each ground cumin, cinnamon, paprika & Cayenne pepper

850ml vegetable stock

10g fresh mint leaves, chopped (optional for garnish)

Making It

Heat the oil in your soup maker if it has a sauté function. Alternatively heat the oil in a saucepan.

Add the onion, garlic, celery and carrot. Sauté for 5 minutes.

Switch off the sauté function on your soup maker/transfer the ingredients to your soup maker.

Add the remaining ingredients to your soup maker, except the mint.

Ensure you don't go above the MAX line in your soup maker. If needed, top up to the MIN line with hot water. Put the lid on and select the chunky setting.

Garnish with the chopped mint leaves (optional).

Aubergine

Serves 4   Calories: (93 per serving)

Ingredients

2 aubergines, cubed

1 medium onion, chopped

1 red pepper, sliced and deseeded

1 carrot (approx. 50g), chopped

½ tsp. dried oregano

½ tsp. dried rosemary

750ml vegetable stock

Making It

Add all ingredients in your soup maker and stir to combine well.

Ensure you don't go above the MAX line in your soup maker. If needed, top up to the MIN line with hot water.

Put the lid on and select the chunky setting.

Carrot & Apricot

Serves 4   Calories: 158 (per serving)

Ingredients

1tbsp olive oil

100g dried apricots

1 medium onion, chopped

6 medium carrots (approx. 300g), chopped

1tbsp clear honey

850ml vegetable stock

Making It

Heat the oil in a saucepan or using the sauté function of your soup maker (if it has one).

Add the chopped onions and gently cook for 2 to 3 minutes, stirring frequently.

Turn off the sauté function/transfer onions to soup maker.

Add all the remaining ingredients apart from the yoghurt. Stir to mix.

Switch the soup maker to the 'smooth' setting.

Once the soup maker has finished add the yoghurt and stir in, or blend manually with the soup maker.

Red Lentil & Carrot

Serves 4   Calories: 133 (per serving)

Ingredients

1 tbsp. olive oil

1 medium onion, chopped finely

6 medium carrots (approx.240g), chopped finely

200g red split lentils, rinsed thoroughly

750ml vegetable stock

Making It

Heat the oil in your soup maker if it has a sauté function or alternatively heat it in a pan on a medium heat.

Add the chopped onion and carrot. Sauté for 5 minutes.

Switch off the sauté function/transfer the carrots and onions to your soup maker.

Add the remaining ingredients and stir to combine well.

Ensure you don't go above the MAX line in your soup maker. If needed, top up to the MIN line with hot water.

Put the lid on and select the chunky setting.

Carrot & Ginger

Serves 4   Calories: 116 (per serving)

Ingredients

1tbsp olive oil

3 tbsp. fresh root ginger, grated

1 medium onion, chopped

10 medium carrots (approx. 600g), peeled & chopped

2 garlic cloves, crushed

750ml vegetable stock

Making It

Heat the oil in a sauce pan or in the base of your soup maker (if you have a soup maker with a sauté function).

Add the chopped onions and garlic and sauté for 2 to 3 minutes, stirring frequently.

Add the grated ginger and carrots and stir for another 2 to 3 minutes.

Switch off the sauté function/transfer onions to soup maker.

Add the vegetable stock, taking care not to go over the MAX line. If required, top up to the MIN line with hot water.

Mix the ingredients around and place the lid on the soup maker. Select the 'Smooth' setting.

Broccoli, Cauliflower and Thyme

Serves 4   Calories: 135 (per serving)

Ingredients

1tbsp olive oil

1 medium onion

3-4 sprigs thyme, leaves only

500g broccoli and cauliflower, chopped

120ml single cream

800ml vegetable stock

Making It

Heat the oil in your soup maker if it has a sauté function/heat oil in a saucepan. Sauté the onions for 2 to 3 minutes.

Switch off the sauté function/transfer onions to soup maker.

Add the thyme leaves, broccoli, cauliflower and vegetable stock, but not the cream. Make sure the ingredients are between the MIN and MAX lines. Top up with hot water if needed.

Set to smooth setting. Once finished, stir in the single cream and blend until mixed.

Garnish with any leftover thyme leaves.

Cauliflower Cheese

Serves 4   Calories: 159 (per serving)

Ingredients

1 tbsp. olive oil

1 small onion, chopped

2 garlic cloves, crushed

1 medium head cauliflower (approx. 450g), chopped into small chunks

1 small potato (approx. 75g), scrubbed and chopped

160g low-fat cheddar cheese, grated

950ml vegetable stock

2 tablespoons fresh basil, chopped (optional for garnish)

Making It

Heat the olive oil in your soup maker if it has a sauté function. Alternatively, heat the oil in a saucepan.

Add the onion and garlic and sauté for about 4-5 minutes.

Switch off the sauté function on your soup maker/transfer onion and garlic to your soup maker.

Add remaining ingredients except cheddar cheese and basil. Stir to combine well.

Ensure you don't go above the MAX line in your soup maker. If needed, top up to the MIN line with hot water.

Put the lid on and select the smooth setting.

Remove the lid and add the cheddar cheese and stir until it is completely melted.

Serve the basil sprinkled on top for garnish.

Curried Parsnip

Serves 4   Calories: 148 (per serving)

Ingredients

1 tbsp. olive oil

1 medium onion, chopped

2 garlic cloves, chopped

½ tbsp. fresh ginger, grated

6 parsnips (approx. 500g.), peeled and chopped

1tsp curry powder

850ml vegetable stock

Making It

Heat the oil in your soup maker if it has a sauté function. Alternatively heat it in a saucepan.

Add the chopped onion and sauté for about 2-3 minutes.

Add the garlic, ginger, curry powder and parsnips and sauté for about 5 minutes.

Switch off the sauté function/transfer to your soup maker.

Add the stock and stir to combine well.

Ensure you don't go above the MAX line in your soup maker. If needed, top up to the MIN line with hot water.

Put the lid on and select the smooth setting.

Asparagus & Pea

Serves 4   Calories: 123 (per serving)

Ingredients

1 tbsp. olive oil

1 medium onion, chopped finely

2 large spring onions, chopped

250g fresh asparagus, trimmed and chopped

250g peas

800ml cups vegetable stock

Making It

Heat the olive oil in your soup maker if it has a sauté function, if not, heat in a saucepan.

Add the onion and spring onions and sauté for about 4-5 minutes.

Add asparagus and sauté for a further 1-2 minutes.

Switch off the sauté function on your soup maker/transfer ingredients to your soup maker.

Add the remaining ingredients and stir to combine well.

Ensure you don't go above the MAX line in your soup maker. If needed, top up to the MIN line with hot water.

Put the lid on and select the smooth setting.

French Onion & Parmesan

Serves 4   Calories: 161 (per serving)

Ingredients

2tbsp olive oil

500g onions, chopped

2 cloves of garlic, crushed

1tbsp flour

2tbsp French mustard

900ml vegetable stock

30g parmesan cheese, grated

Making It

Heat the oil in your soup maker if it has a sauté function. Alternatively, heat the oil in a saucepan.

Add the chopped onions and sauté for 5 minutes. Add the crushed garlic and sauté for a further 2 to 3 minutes.

Switch the sauté feature off/transfer ingredients to your soup maker.

Add all the remaining ingredients, apart from the parmesan, to your soup maker and stir to combine.

Ensure you don't go above the MAX line in your soup maker. If needed, top up to the MIN line with hot water.

Put the lid on and select the chunky setting.

Remove the lid and add the parmesan, stir in until melted.

Creamy Spinach

Serves 4   Calories: 141 (per serving)

Ingredients

1tbsp olive oil

1 medium onion, chopped

1 medium potato (approx. 100g), scrubbed and chopped

400g spinach leaves

800ml vegetable stock

100ml single cream

Making It

Heat the oil in your soup maker if it has the sauté function. Alternatively, heat the oil in a saucepan.

Add the chopped onions and sauté for 5 minutes.

Switch the sauté feature off/transfer ingredients to your soup maker.

Add all the remaining ingredients, apart from the cream, to your soup maker and stir to combine.

Ensure you don't go above the MAX line in your soup maker. If needed, top up to the MIN line with hot water.

Put the lid on and select the smooth setting.

Remove the lid and add the single cream, stir in or blend with the soup maker's manual blend setting.

Watercress & Potato

Serves 4   Calories: 212 (per serving)

Ingredients

600g potatoes, peeled and thinly sliced

2tbsp olive oil

100g fresh watercress

1 litre vegetable stock

Making It

Heat the oil in your soup maker if it has a sauté function. If not, heat the oil in a saucepan.

Add the sliced potatoes and sauté for about 5 minutes, stirring frequently.

Switch the sauté feature off/transfer potatoes to your soup maker.

Add the vegetable stock, but not the watercress.

Ensure you don't go above the MAX line in your soup maker. If needed, top up to the MIN line with hot water.

Put the lid on and select the smooth setting.

Remove the lid and add the watercress. Use the manual blend function for about 20 to 30 seconds to blend together.

Chilled Avocado & Cucumber

Serves 4   Calories: 200 (per serving)

Ingredients

2 medium ripe avocados

100g cucumber, sliced

2tbsp lemon juice

900ml skimmed milk

Mint leaves for garnish (optional)

Making It

Cut the avocados in half and scoop the flesh out. Add all the ingredients to the soup maker jug.

Place the lid back on and select the 'blend' or 'juice' function on your soup maker – refer to your manufacturer's instruction manual for the correct mode. On the Morphy Richards Soup Maker you select the 'juice' setting.

Once blended, garnish with mint leaves (optional).

Leek & Carrot

Serves 4   Calories: 96

Ingredients

1tbsp olive oil

200g carrots, peeled and sliced

500g leeks (about 3), sliced

3tbsp fresh parsley, chopped

800ml vegetable stock

Making It

Heat the oil in your soup maker if it has a sauté function. If not, heat the oil in a saucepan.

Add the sliced leeks and carrots and sauté for about 5 minutes, stirring frequently.

Switch the sauté feature off/transfer the leeks and carrots to your soup maker.

Add the vegetable stock, but not the parsley to your soup maker.

Ensure you don't go above the MAX line in your soup maker. If needed, top up to the MIN line with hot water.

Put the lid on and select the smooth setting.

Remove the lid and stir in the chopped parsley.

Tomato & Celery

Serves 4   Calories: 108 (per serving)

Ingredients

1tbsp olive oil

2 red onions, chopped

1 garlic clove, crushed

400g can of chopped tomatoes

500g (approx. 13 sticks) celery, chopped

750ml vegetable stock

Making It

Heat the oil in your soup maker if it has a sauté function. If not, heat the oil in a saucepan.

Add the chopped onions, celery and garlic and sauté for about 5 minutes, stirring frequently.

Switch the sauté feature off/transfer the ingredients to your soup maker.

Add the vegetable stock and chopped tomatoes to your soup maker.

Ensure you don't go above the MAX line in your soup maker. If needed, top up to the MIN line with hot water.

Put the lid on and select the smooth setting.

Garlic, Lentil & Tomato

Serves 4   Calories: 149 (per serving)

Ingredients

2tbsp olive oil

1 medium onion, chopped

4 cloves garlic, crushed

150g split red lentils, washed

400g tin chopped tomatoes

850ml vegetable stock

Making It

Heat the oil in your soup maker if it has a sauté function. If not, heat the oil in a saucepan.

Add the chopped onions and garlic and sauté for about 5 minutes, stirring frequently.

Switch the sauté feature off/transfer the ingredients to your soup maker.

Add the remaining ingredients to your soup maker.

Ensure you don't go above the MAX line in your soup maker. If needed, top up to the MIN line with hot water.

Put the lid on and select the smooth setting.

Pea and Mint

Serves 4   Calories: 186 (per serving)

Ingredients

450g peas

1 medium potato (approx. 100g), scrubbed and chopped

30g fresh mint, chopped

2tbsp crème fraiche

850ml vegetable stock

Making It

Add all the ingredients to your soup maker apart from the crème fraiche.

Ensure you don't go above the MAX line in your soup maker. If needed, top up to the MIN line with hot water.

Put the lid on and select the smooth setting.

Once the program has finished, lift the lid and add the crème fraiche. Blend for around 15-20 seconds.

Potato, Parsnip & Leek

Serves 4   Calories: 200 (per serving)

Ingredients

1tbsp. olive oil

1 medium onion, chopped

1 garlic clove, crushed

½ tbsp. fresh ginger, grated

2 leeks (approx. 350g), sliced

3 parsnips (approx. 240g), chopped

2 potatoes (approx. 200g), scrubbed and chopped

900ml vegetable stock

Making It

Heat the oil in your soup maker if it has a sauté function. If not, heat the oil in a saucepan.

Add the chopped onions and sauté for about 5 minutes, stirring frequently. Add the crushed garlic and ginger and sauté for a further 2 to 3 minutes.

Switch the sauté feature off/transfer the ingredients to your soup maker.

Add the remaining ingredients to your soup maker.

Ensure you don't go above the MAX line in your soup maker. If needed, top up to the MIN line with hot water.

Put the lid on and select the smooth setting.

Brussel Sprout & Cheddar

Serves 4   Calories: 216 (per serving)

Ingredients

1 tbsp. olive oil

1 medium onion, chopped

500g Brussels sprouts, trimmed and halved

2 garlic cloves, crushed

850ml vegetable stock

125g low-fat cheddar cheese, grated

Making It

Heat the oil in your soup maker if it has a sauté function. If not, heat the oil in a saucepan.

Add the chopped onions and garlic and sauté for about 5 minutes, stirring frequently.

Switch the sauté feature off/transfer the ingredients to your soup maker.

Add the remaining ingredients, except the cheddar cheese, to your soup maker.

Ensure you don't go above the MAX line in your soup maker. If needed, top up to the MIN line with hot water.

Put the lid on and select the smooth setting.

Remove the lid and stir in the cheddar cheese until melted.

Carrot & Parsnip

Serves 4   Calories: 154 (per serving)

Ingredients

2 tbsp. olive oil

1 medium onion, chopped

2 garlic cloves, crushed

240g parsnips, peeled and chopped

240g carrots, peeled and chopped

900ml vegetable stock

Making It

Heat the oil in your soup maker if it has a sauté function. If not, heat the oil in a saucepan.

Add the chopped onions and garlic and sauté for about 5 minutes, stirring frequently. Add the parsnips and carrots and sauté for a further 5 minutes.

Switch the sauté feature off/transfer the ingredients to your soup maker.

Add the remaining ingredients to your soup maker.

Ensure you don't go above the MAX line in your soup maker. If needed, top up to the MIN line with hot water.

Put the lid on and select the smooth setting.

Sweet Potato & Coconut

Serves 1   Calories: 176

Ingredients

1tbsp olive oil

1 medium onion, sliced

2 cloves garlic, crushed

300g sweet potato, peeled and chopped

250ml reduced fat coconut milk

2tsp ground coriander

700ml vegetable stock

Making It

Heat the oil in your soup maker if it has a sauté function. Alternatively heat the oil in a saucepan.

Add the chopped onions and sauté for 5 minutes. Add the garlic, sweet potato and coriander and sauté for a further 2 to 3 minutes, stirring frequently.

Switch off the sauté function on your soup maker/transfer ingredients to your soup maker.

Add the remaining ingredients. Ensure you are between the MIN and MAX lines on your soup maker. Add more hot water if required.

Set on smooth function.

Beetroot & Apple

Serves 4   Calories: 136 (per serving)

Ingredients

3 raw beetroot (approx. 450g), scrubbed, peeled and chopped

1 Bramley apple (approx. 220g), peeled, cored and chopped

1 medium onion, chopped

Juice from half a lemon

850ml vegetable stock

3tbsp crème fraiche

Making It

Cook the cubed beetroot in a saucepan of boiling water, covered, for about 15 to 20 minutes. When ready, keep the water to put it in your soup maker.

Alternatively you can buy cooked beetroot – just check what it has been cooked in.

Add the cooked beetroot and all the remaining ingredients, except the crème fraiche, to your soup maker.

Ensure you don't go over the MAX line in your soup maker. If needed, top up to the MIN line with hot water.

Put the lid on and select the smooth setting.

When complete, add the crème fraiche and manually blend for 20 to 30 seconds.

Caribbean Pumpkin

Serves 4   Calories: 110 (per serving)

Ingredients

400g pumpkin, skinned and chopped

2 large carrots (approx.240g), peeled and chopped

150g sweet potato, scrubbed and chopped

1 medium onion, chopped

1 scotch bonnet (or red chilli), seeded and sliced

2 tsp. fresh orange zest, grated finely

1tsp dried thyme

2 bay leaves

1tsp ground cinnamon

¼ tsp. ground nutmeg

850ml vegetable stock

Making It

Add all the ingredients to your soup maker and stir to combine well.

Ensure you don't go above the MAX line in your soup maker. If needed, top up to the MIN line with hot water.

Put the lid on and select the chunky setting.

Discard the bay leaves before serving.

Carrot & Orange

Serves 4   Calories: 138 (per serving)

Ingredients

600g carrots, peeled and chopped

1 onion, chopped

600ml vegetable stock

300ml fresh orange juice

3tbsp crème fraiche

Making It

Add all ingredients except the orange juice and crème fraiche to your soup maker and stir to combine well.

Ensure you don't go above the MAX line in your soup maker. If needed, top up to the MIN line with hot water.

Put the lid on and select the smooth setting.

Remove the lid and stir in the orange juice and crème fraiche. Manually blend for 10 to 20 seconds.

Courgette & Pea

Serves 4   Calories: 121 (per serving)

Ingredients

2 courgettes (approx.300g), chopped finely

200g peas

1 medium onion, chopped finely

900ml vegetable stock

3 tbsp. crème fraiche

Making It

Add all ingredients to your soup maker and stir to combine well.

Ensure you don't go above the MAX line in your soup maker. If needed, top up to the MIN line with hot water.

Put the lid on and select the chunky setting.

Leek & Butternut Squash

Serves 4   Calories: 261 (per serving)

Ingredients

600g butternut squash, peeled, seeded and chopped finely

2 leeks (approx.400g), chopped

1 medium onion, chopped

2 garlic cloves, crushed

2tsp mixed dried herbs

750ml vegetable stock

70g plain Greek yogurt

Making It

Add all ingredients except the yoghurt to your soup maker and stir to combine well.

Ensure you don't go above the MAX line in your soup maker. If needed, top up to the MIN line with hot water.

Put the lid on and select the smooth setting.

Remove the lid and mix the yoghurt in, blending manually for about 15 to 20 seconds.

Spiced Root Vegetable Medley

Serves 4   Calories: 126 (per serving)

Ingredients

1 tbsp. olive oil

1 onion, chopped

2 cloves garlic, crushed

300g carrots, peeled and chopped

150g parsnips, peeled and chopped

400g swede, peeled and chopped

2tsp garam masala

750ml vegetable stock

Making It

Heat the oil in your soup maker if it has a sauté function. Alternatively heat the oil in a saucepan.

Add the chopped onions and sauté for 5 minutes. Add the garlic and garam masala and sauté for a further 2 minutes.

Switch off the sauté function on your soup maker/transfer the ingredients to your soup maker.

Add all the remaining ingredients to your soup maker and stir to combine.

Ensure you don't go above the MAX line in your soup maker. If needed, top up to the MIN line with hot water.

Put the lid on and select the smooth setting.

Curried Carrot & Chickpea

Serves 4   Calories: 291 (per serving)

Ingredients

1 tbsp. olive oil

1 red onion, chopped

3 stalks celery, chopped

600g carrots (approx.6), peeled and chopped

400g tin of cooked chickpeas, drained

2 tsp. garam masala

1tbsp. fresh root ginger, grated

850ml vegetable stock

Making It

Heat the oil in your soup maker if it has a sauté function. Alternatively heat the oil in a saucepan.

Add the chopped onions, ginger, celery, garlic and garam masala and sauté for 5 minutes, stirring frequently.

Switch off the sauté function on your soup maker/transfer the ingredients to your soup maker.

Add the remaining ingredients to your soup maker and stir to combine.

Ensure you don't go above the MAX line in your soup maker. If needed, top up to the MIN line with hot water.

Put the lid on and select the chunky setting.

Carrot & Coriander

Serves 4   Calories: 174 (per serving)

Ingredients

1 tbsp. olive oil

1 small onion, chopped

600g carrots (approx. 6 large carrots), peeled and chopped

2 tsp. ground coriander

800ml vegetable stock

150ml single cream

1 tbsp. fresh coriander, chopped (optional for garnish)

Making It

Heat the oil in your soup maker if it has a sauté function. Alternatively heat the oil in a saucepan. Add the chopped onions and sauté for 5 minutes.

Switch off the sauté function on your soup maker/transfer the ingredients to your soup maker.

Add the remaining ingredients, except the cream and fresh coriander, and stir to combine well.

Ensure you don't go above the MAX line in your soup maker. If needed, top up to the MIN line with hot water.

Put the lid on and select the smooth setting.

Once complete, remove the lid and mix the cream in using the manual blend setting. Garnish with chopped fresh coriander (optional).

Red Lentil & Kale

Serves 4   Calories: 90 (per serving)

Ingredients

1tbsp olive oil

1 onion, chopped

2 cloves garlic, crushed

1tsp mild chilli powder

80g kale

100g red split lentils, washed

850ml vegetable stock

Making It

Heat the oil in your soup maker if it has a sauté function. Alternatively heat the oil in a saucepan.

Add the chopped onions, garlic and chilli powder and sauté for 5 minutes, stirring frequently.

Switch off the sauté function on your soup maker/transfer the ingredients to your soup maker.

Add the remaining ingredients to your soup maker and stir to combine.

Ensure you don't go above the MAX line in your soup maker. If needed, top up to the MIN line with hot water.

Put the lid on and select the smooth setting.

Red Pepper & Lime

Serves 4   Calories: 121 (per serving)

Ingredients

1tbsp olive oil

4 red peppers, deseeded and chopped

Zest and juice of 1 lime

1 medium onion, chopped

1 garlic clove, crushed

1 red chilli, sliced (deseed if you prefer a mild taste)

3tbsp tomato puree

900ml vegetable or chicken stock

Making It

Heat the oil in your soup maker if it has a sauté function. Alternatively heat the oil in a saucepan. Add the chopped onions, garlic and peppers. Sauté for 5 minutes, stirring frequently.

Switch off the sauté function on your soup maker/transfer the ingredients to your soup maker.

Add the remaining ingredients, reserving a little lime zest, to your soup maker and stir to combine.

Ensure you don't go above the MAX line in your soup maker. If needed, top up to the MIN line with hot water.

Put the lid on and select the smooth setting. Garnish with the reserved lime zest.

Red Onion & Beetroot

Serves 4   Calories: 180 (per serving)

Ingredients

1tbsp olive oil

350g red onions, sliced

300g cooked beetroot, cut into sticks

2 garlic cloves, crushed

75g small shell pasta

900ml vegetable stock

2tbsp chopped chives (optional for garnish)

Making It

Heat the oil in your soup maker if it has a sauté function. Alternatively heat the oil in a saucepan.

Add the chopped onions and garlic and sauté for 5 minutes, stirring frequently.

Switch off the sauté function on your soup maker/transfer the ingredients to your soup maker.

Add the remaining ingredients to your soup maker and stir to combine.

Ensure you don't go above the MAX line in your soup maker. If needed, top up to the MIN line with hot water.

Put the lid on and select the chunky setting.

Garnish with chopped chives (optional).

Cannellini & Tomato

Serves 4   Calories: 245 (per serving)

Ingredients

2tbsp olive oil

1 small carrot (approx.70g), peeled and chopped finely

1 celery stick (approx.40g), chopped finely

1 medium onion, chopped finely

2 garlic cloves, crushed

150g canned cannellini beans, rinsed and drained

400g can chopped tomatoes

100g tiny pasta shells

1tsp mixed dried herbs

2 bay leaves

900ml vegetable stock

Making It

Add all ingredients to your soup maker and stir to combine well.

Ensure you don't go above the MAX line in your soup maker. If needed, top up to the MIN line with hot water.

Put the lid on and select the chunky setting.

Leek & Potato

Serves 4   Calories: 344 (per serving)

Ingredients

450g potatoes (approx. 3), scrubbed & chopped

500g leeks (approx. 3), chopped

120g carrot, chopped

1tsp mixed dried herbs

850ml vegetable stock

3tbsp crème fraiche

Making It

Add all ingredients to your soup maker, except the crème fraiche and stir to combine well.

Ensure you don't go above the MAX line in your soup maker. If needed, top up to the MIN line with hot water.

Put the lid on and select the smooth setting.

When the program has finished, stir in the crème fraiche and blend using the manual setting for 15 to 20 seconds.

Simple Tomato Soup

Serves 4   Calories: 158 (per serving)

Ingredients

1tbsp olive oil

1 onion, chopped

2 garlic cloves, crushed

1 potato (approx. 100g)

1tsp mixed dried herbs

2 x 400g tin plum peeled tomatoes

850ml vegetable stock

Making It

Add all ingredients to your soup maker. Stir to combine well.

Ensure you don't go above the MAX line in your soup maker. If needed, top up to the MIN line with hot water.

Put the lid on and select the smooth setting.

Pumpkin, Pepper & Coriander

Serves 4   Calories: 105 (per serving)

Ingredients

1tbsp olive oil

400g pumpkin, deseeded and cut into chunks

2 red peppers, deseeded and sliced

1 onion, chopped

3 cloves garlic, crushed

2 red chillies, deseeded and finely sliced

3tbsp fresh coriander, chopped

1tsp paprika

2tbsp crème fraiche

850ml vegetable stock

Making It

Add all ingredients to your soup maker, except the coriander and crème fraiche. Stir to combine well.

Ensure you don't go above the MAX line in your soup maker. If needed, top up to the MIN line with hot water.

Put the lid on and select the smooth setting.

Add the chopped coriander and crème fraiche. Manually blend for 15 to 20 seconds.

Courgette & Spinach

Serves 4   Calories: 148 (per serving)

Ingredients

1tbsp olive oil

1 medium onion, chopped

2 garlic cloves, crushed

150g spinach

200g courgettes, sliced

1 medium potato, scrubbed & chopped

2tsp mixed dried herbs

850ml vegetable stock

Making It

Heat the oil in your soup maker if it has a sauté function. Alternatively heat the oil in a saucepan.

Add the onion and sauté for about 5 minutes. Add the garlic and courgettes and sauté for a further 5 minutes.

Switch off the sauté function on your soup maker/transfer the ingredients to your soup maker.

Add all the remaining ingredients to your soup maker.

Ensure you don't go above the MAX line in your soup maker. If needed, top up to the MIN line with hot water.

Put the lid on and select the smooth setting.

Carrot & Apple

Ingredients

1tbsp olive oil

500g carrots, chopped

1 medium onion, chopped

1 Bramley cooking apple, chopped and core removed

850ml vegetable stock

Making It

Heat the oil in your soup maker if it has a sauté function. Alternatively heat the oil in a saucepan.

Add the chopped onion. Sauté for 5 minutes, stirring frequently.

Switch off the sauté function on your soup maker/transfer the ingredients to your soup maker.

Add the remaining ingredients to your soup maker and stir to combine.

Ensure you don't go above the MAX line in your soup maker. If needed, top up to the MIN line with hot water.

Put the lid on and select the smooth setting.

Broccoli & Almond

Serves 4   Calories: 167 (per serving)

Ingredients

1tbsp olive oil

500g broccoli, roughly chopped

50g ground almonds

3 cloves garlic, crushed

1 medium onion, chopped

1 small carrot, chopped

850ml vegetable stock

Making It

Heat the oil in your soup maker if it has a sauté function. Alternatively heat the oil in a saucepan. Add the chopped onions and garlic. Sauté for 5 minutes, stirring frequently.

Switch off the sauté function on your soup maker/transfer the ingredients to your soup maker.

Add the remaining ingredients to your soup maker, except the ground almonds. Stir to combine.

Ensure you don't go above the MAX line in your soup maker. If needed, top up to the MIN line with hot water.

Put the lid on and select the smooth setting.

Once finished, add the ground almonds and use the blend setting for 15 to 20 seconds.

Cannellini & Kale Soup

Serves 4   Calories: 160 (per serving)

Ingredients

1tbsp olive oil

1 medium onion, chopped

2 garlic cloves, crushed

80g kale, chopped

400g can of cannellini beans, drained and rinsed

2 tsp. dried mixed herbs

850ml vegetable stock

Making It

Heat the oil in your soup maker if it has a sauté function. Alternatively heat the oil in a saucepan.

Add the chopped onions and garlic. Sauté for 5 minutes, stirring frequently.

Switch off the sauté function on your soup maker/transfer the ingredients to your soup maker.

Add the remaining ingredients to your soup maker and stir to combine.

Ensure you don't go above the MAX line in your soup maker. If needed, top up to the MIN line with hot water.

Put the lid on and select the smooth setting.

Tomato & Basil

Serves 4   Calories: 90 (per serving)

Ingredients

3 shallots (approx. 45g), chopped

2 garlic cloves, peeled and crushed

5 medium fresh tomatoes (approx. 440g), chopped

1 potato (approx. 100g), scrubbed and chopped

1 carrot (approx. 60g), scrubbed and chopped

750ml vegetable stock

8 large fresh basil leaves, chopped

2 large fresh basil leaves for garnish, chopped

Making It

Add all ingredients except the basil to your soup maker and stir to combine.

Ensure you don't go above the MAX line in your soup maker. If needed, top up to the MIN line with hot water.

Put the lid on and select the smooth setting.

Remove the lid and mix the basil using the manual blend setting. Garnish with chopped basil leaves.

Lettuce Soup

Serves 4   Calories: 116 (per serving)

Ingredients

1tbsp olive oil

1 medium onion, chopped

2 garlic cloves, crushed

1 potato (approx. 100g), scrubbed and chopped

1 romaine lettuce, leaves torn

3tbsp fresh parsley, chopped (optional for garnish)

950ml vegetable stock

Making It

Heat the oil in your soup maker if it has a sauté function. Alternatively heat the oil in a saucepan.

Add the chopped onions and garlic. Sauté for 5 minutes, stirring frequently.

Switch off the sauté function on your soup maker/transfer the ingredients to your soup maker.

Add the remaining ingredients, except the parsley, to your soup maker and stir to combine.

Ensure you don't go above the MAX line in your soup maker. If needed, top up to the MIN line with hot water.

Put the lid on and select the smooth setting.

Garnish with chopped parsley (optional).

Spinach & Coconut

Serves 4   Calories: 146 (per serving)

Ingredients

1tbsp olive oil

1 medium onion, chopped

2 garlic cloves, crushed

450g spinach leaves

400ml coconut milk

2tbsp Thai green curry paste

Juice of 1 lime

800ml vegetable stock

Making It

Heat the oil in your soup maker if it has a sauté function. Alternatively heat the oil in a saucepan.

Add the chopped onions and garlic. Sauté for 5 minutes, stirring frequently.

Switch off the sauté function on your soup maker/transfer the ingredients to your soup maker.

Add the remaining ingredients to your soup maker and stir to combine.

Ensure you don't go above the MAX line in your soup maker. If needed, top up to the MIN line with hot water.

Put the lid on and select the smooth setting.

Broccoli & Stilton

Serves 4   Calories: 204 (per serving)

Ingredients

1tbsp. olive oil

1 medium onion, chopped

4 large spring onions, chopped

1 medium celery stalk, chopped

350g fresh broccoli, chopped

1 medium potato (approx. 100g), scrubbed and chopped

850ml vegetable stock

50g stilton, cubed

Making It

Heat the oil in your soup maker if it has a sauté function. Alternatively heat the oil in a saucepan. Add the chopped onions, garlic, celery and spring onion. Sauté for 5 minutes, stirring frequently.

Switch off the sauté function on your soup maker/transfer the ingredients to your soup maker.

Add the remaining ingredients to your soup maker, except the stilton. Stir to combine.

Ensure you don't go above the MAX line in your soup maker. If needed, top up to the MIN line with hot water.

Put the lid on and select the smooth setting. When finished remove the lid and add the stilton and stir until completely melted.

Roasted Tomato & Pepper

Serves 4   Calories: 120 (per serving)

Ingredients

1tbsp olive oil

1 medium onion, chopped

2 garlic cloves, crushed

500g fresh tomatoes, chopped

3 medium red bell peppers, seeded and chopped roughly

1 celery stalk, chopped finely

2tbsp tomato puree

900ml vegetable stock

Fresh basil, chopped (optional, for garnish)

Making It

Preheat the oven to 190°C/Gas Mark 5. Put the chopped tomatoes and peppers on a baking tray. Drizzle 1 tablespoon of olive oil over them.

Roast for about 25 minutes.

Remove the tomatoes and bell peppers from the oven and add to your soup maker, together with the remaining ingredients.

Ensure you don't go above the MAX line in your soup maker. If needed, top up to the MIN line with hot water.

Put the lid on and select the smooth setting. Serve with chopped basil for garnish (optional).

Cream of Asparagus

Serves 4   Calories: 242 (per serving)

Ingredients

1tbsp olive oil

400g fresh asparagus, cut into 2cm pieces

1 medium onion, chopped

1 clove garlic, crushed

1 medium potato, peeled and diced

2 sticks celery, finely sliced

2tbsp plain flour

150ml single cream

850ml vegetable stock

Making It

Heat the oil in your soup maker if it has a sauté function. Alternatively heat the oil in a saucepan.

Add the chopped onions, garlic, celery and asparagus. Sauté for 5 minutes, stirring frequently. Add the flour and combine. Sauté for a further 2 to 3 minutes.

Switch off the sauté function on your soup maker/transfer the ingredients to your soup maker.

Add the remaining ingredients to your soup maker, except the single cream.

Ensure you don't go above the MAX line in your soup maker. If needed, top up to the MIN line with hot water.

Put the lid on and select the smooth setting.

Lift the lid and stir in the single cream. Blend manually for 15 to 20 seconds.

Sweet Potato & Orange

Serves 4   Calories: 249 (per serving)

Ingredients

1 tbsp. olive oil

500g sweet potatoes, peeled and diced

1 large carrot, peeled and sliced

1 medium onion, sliced

350ml freshly squeezed orange juice

750ml vegetable stock

3tbsp crème fraiche

Making It

Heat the oil in your soup maker if it has a sauté function. Alternatively heat the oil in a saucepan.

Add the chopped onions. Sauté for 5 minutes, stirring frequently. Add the sweet potato and carrot and sauté for a further 5 minutes.

Switch off the sauté function on your soup maker/transfer the ingredients to your soup maker.

Add the remaining ingredients to your soup maker, except the crème fraiche.

Ensure you don't go above the MAX line in your soup maker. If needed, top up to the MIN line with hot water.

Put the lid on and select the chunky setting.

Lift the lid, stir in the crème fraiche and mix through.

Great Green Soup

Serves 4   Calories: 242 (per serving)

Ingredients

1tbsp olive oil

1 red onion, chopped

2 garlic cloves, crushed

3 sticks celery, chopped

1 courgette, chopped

10 broccoli florets, chopped

60g baby spinach leaves

60g kale leaves

60g cabbage

1 medium potato, scrubbed and chopped

850ml vegetable stock

Making It

Heat the oil in your soup maker if it has a sauté function. Alternatively heat the oil in a saucepan.

Add the onions and garlic. Sauté for 5 minutes. Stirring frequently.

Switch off the sauté function on your soup maker/transfer the ingredients to your soup maker.

Add the remaining ingredients to your soup maker.

Ensure you don't go above the MAX line in your soup maker. If needed, top up to the MIN line with hot water.

Put the lid on and select the smooth setting.

Pear & Parsnip

Serves 4   Calories: 160 (per serving)

Ingredients

1tbsp olive oil

1 red onion, chopped

3 pears, peeled, cored and chopped

3 parsnips, peeled and chopped

1tsp ground cinnamon

1tsp ground nutmeg

850ml vegetable stock

Making It

Add all the ingredients to your soup maker.

Ensure you don't go above the MAX line in your soup maker. If needed, top up to the MIN line with hot water.

Put the lid on and select the smooth setting.

Creamy Mushroom Soup

Serves 4   Calories: 131 (per serving)

Ingredients

350g mushrooms, sliced into chunks

3 cloves garlic, crushed

2 medium red onions, chopped

200ml single cream

900ml vegetable stock

Making It

Heat the oil in your soup maker if it has a sauté function. Alternatively heat the oil in a saucepan.

Add the onions and garlic. Sauté for 5 minutes. Stirring frequently. Add the mushrooms and sauté for a further 5 minutes.

Switch off the sauté function on your soup maker/transfer the ingredients to your soup maker.

Add the remaining ingredients, except the single cream, to your soup maker.

Ensure you don't go above the MAX line in your soup maker. If needed, top up to the MIN line with hot water.

Put the lid on and select the smooth setting.

Lift the lid and stir in the single cream. Manually blend for 15 to 20 seconds.

Courgette & Garlic

Serves 4   Calories: 111 (per serving)

Ingredients

1 tbsp. olive oil

450g courgettes, chopped

5 garlic cloves, crushed

1 potato (approx. 100g), scrubbed and diced

750ml vegetable stock

Making It

Heat the oil in the soup maker or saucepan.

Add the crushed garlic and chopped courgettes and sauté for around 5 minutes.

Switch the sauté function off/transfer ingredients to your soup maker.

Add the potato and vegetable stock. Ensure you don't go over the MAX line. If needed add some more hot water to reach the MIN line.

Set the soup maker on the smooth setting.

Cauliflower & Spinach

Serves 4   Calories: 124 (per serving)

Ingredients

1 medium onion, chopped

1 cauliflower (about 600g), broken into florets

2 garlic cloves, crushed

1tsp ground coriander

150g fresh spinach leaves

750ml vegetable stock

3tbsp crème fraiche

Making It

Heat the oil in your soup maker if it has a sauté function. Alternatively heat the oil in a saucepan.

Add the onion and garlic and sauté for 5 minutes.

Switch off the sauté function on your soup maker/transfer the ingredients to your soup maker.

Add the remaining ingredients, except the crème fraiche, to your soup maker.

Ensure you don't go above the MAX line in your soup maker. If needed, top up to the MIN line with hot water.

Put the lid on and select the smooth setting.

Lift the lid and stir in the crème fraiche. Use the manual blend setting for 15 to 20 seconds.

Gazpacho

Serves 4   Calories: 258 (per serving)

Ingredients

600g ripe fresh tomatoes, chopped

400ml tomato juice

1tsp ground cumin

1 small cucumber (approx. 200g), chopped

1 red pepper, deseeded and chopped

1 red onion, chopped

3 cloves garlic, crushed

3tbsp. red wine vinegar

90ml olive oil

100ml chilled water

Making It

Add all ingredients in your soup maker and stir to combine well.

Put the lid on and select the juice setting.

Remove the lid and transfer the gazpacho in a large container or jug.

Refrigerate, covered for about 3 hours to chill before serving.

Roasted Aubergine & Pepper

Serves 4   Calories: 143 (per serving)

Ingredients

1 tbsp. olive oil

1 aubergine, chopped

2 red peppers, deseeded and chopped

2 garlic cloves, sliced

2 red onions, sliced

400g can chopped tomatoes

1 red chilli, sliced (deseed if you prefer a milder taste)

750ml vegetable stock

Making It

Preheat the oven to 375°F /190°C. Put the chopped aubergine, sliced garlic and chopped red peppers on a baking tray. Drizzle 1 tablespoon of olive oil over them.

Roast for about 15 minutes.

Remove from the oven and add to your soup maker, together with the remaining ingredients.

Ensure you don't go above the MAX line in your soup maker. If needed, top up to the MIN line with hot water.

Put the lid on and select the smooth setting.

Plum & Tomato Soup

Serves 4   Calories: 149 (per serving)

Ingredients

1tbsp olive oil

500g red plums

400g can of chopped tomatoes

Juice of half a lemon

100ml tomato juice

1tsp mixed spice

750ml vegetable stock

Making It

Add all the ingredients to your soup maker. Mix together.

Ensure you don't go above the MAX line in your soup maker. If needed, top up to the MIN line with hot water.

Select the smooth setting.

Spicy Green Soup

Serves 4   Calories: 178 (per serving)

Ingredients

1 green cabbage, chopped

1 courgette, chopped

180g broccoli florets, chopped

1 red pepper, seeded and chopped

1 red chilli, seeded and chopped

1 tbsp. fresh parsley, chopped

1 tbsp. fresh thyme chopped

750ml vegetable stock

Making It

Add all ingredients to your soup maker and stir to combine well.

Ensure you don't go above the MAX line in your soup maker. If needed, top up to the MIN line with hot water.

Put the lid on and select the smooth setting.

Courgette & Mint Soup

Serves 4   Calories: 60 (per serving)

Ingredients

3 large courgettes, chopped

1 medium onion, chopped

10g fresh mint, chopped

750ml vegetable stock

Making It

Add all ingredients to your soup maker and stir to combine well.

Ensure you don't go above the MAX line in your soup maker. If needed, top up to the MIN line with hot water.

Put the lid on and select the smooth setting.

TIP: Also tastes good served chilled.

Curried Banana

Serves 4   Calories: 241 (per serving)

Ingredients

1tbsp olive oil

1 medium onion chopped

2 cloves garlic crushed

1 red chilli finely, sliced

1tsp fresh root ginger, grated

Pinch each of turmeric, cumin & coriander

1 lime juice

2 bananas peeled & chopped

100g Basmati rice

200ml coconut milk

750ml vegetable stock

Making It

Heat oil in the soup maker (if it has a sauté function), if not, use a saucepan.

Sauté the chopped onion for 3 minutes, stirring frequently.

Add the crushed garlic, grated ginger, sliced chilli and ground spices. Sauté for a further 2 minutes.

Turn off the sauté feature on your soup maker/remove saucepan and add ingredients to your soup maker.

Add the rice, coconut milk and stock. Stir round to mix. If your mixture does not reach the Min level on your soup maker add some more boiling water until it does. Make sure you don't go over the MAX line.

Set the soup maker setting to smooth setting.

When the soup maker has finished take off the lid and add the chopped banana and lime juice. Manually blend for 20 to 30 seconds or until smooth.

Red Pepper & Peanut Soup

Serves 4   Calories: 303 (per serving)

Ingredients

1tbsp olive oil

1 medium onion, chopped

2 red peppers, deseeded and chopped

3 cloves garlic, crushed

400g can chopped tomatoes

1 red chilli, sliced (deseed if you prefer)

125g peanut butter

800ml vegetable stock

Making It

Heat the oil in your soup maker if it has a sauté function. Alternatively heat the oil in a saucepan.

Add the onion and garlic. Sauté for about 5 minutes.

Switch off the sauté function on your soup maker/transfer the ingredients to your soup maker.

Add the remaining ingredients to your soup maker.

Ensure you don't go above the MAX line in your soup maker. If needed, top up to the MIN line with hot water.

Put the lid on and select the smooth setting.

Butternut Squash & Chestnut

Serves 4   Calories: 256 (per serving)

Ingredients

1tbsp olive oil

1 butternut squash, peeled and chopped

180g chestnuts, peeled and cooked

1 red onion

2 cloves garlic, crushed

400g chopped tomatoes

1tsp ground cinnamon

1tsp ground ginger

1 red chilli, sliced (remove seeds if you prefer)

800ml vegetable stock

Making It

Try and buy vacuum-packed chestnuts that have already been peeled and cooked (they sell them in most supermarkets). It will save you the time of roasting them and removing their skin! If you can't get any, roast them in the oven for around 15-20 minutes and then remove their shells (score an X on the base of each one before roasting).

Heat the oil in your soup maker if it has a sauté function. Alternatively heat the oil in a saucepan.

Add the onion, garlic and chilli. Sauté for about 5 minutes. Add the ginger and cinnamon and sauté for a further 1 or 2 minutes.

Switch off the sauté function on your soup maker/transfer the ingredients to your soup maker.

Add the remaining ingredients to your soup maker.

Ensure you don't go above the MAX line in your soup maker. If needed, top up to the MIN line with hot water.

Put the lid on and select the smooth setting.

Celery & Cashew

Serves 4   Calories: 252 (per serving)

Ingredients

1tbsp olive oil

1 medium onion, chopped

1 potato (approx. 100g), scrubbed and chopped

1 head celery, chopped

90g cashew nuts, chopped

850ml vegetable stock

Making It

Heat the oil in your soup maker if it has a sauté function. Alternatively heat the oil in a saucepan.

Add the onions and sauté for about 5 minutes. Add the potato, celery and nuts. Sauté for a further 5 minutes, stirring frequently.

Switch off the sauté function on your soup maker/transfer the ingredients to your soup maker.

Add all the remaining ingredients to your soup maker. Stir the ingredients.

Ensure you don't go above the MAX line in your soup maker. If needed, top up to the MIN line with hot water.

Put the lid on and select the smooth setting.

Spiced Cauliflower

Serves 4   Calories: 190 (per serving)

Ingredients

1tbsp olive oil

1 cauliflower, chopped

100g potatoes, scrubbed and chopped

1 medium onion, chopped

2 garlic cloves, crushed

1 red chilli, sliced (deseed if you prefer a milder taste)

1tsp each of ground coriander, cumin and turmeric

850ml vegetable stock

Making It

Heat the olive oil in your soup maker if it has a sauté function. If not, heat in a pan.

Add the chopped onion and sauté for 2 to 3 minutes. Add the garlic, ground spices, chilli and chopped cauliflower and continue to sauté for a further 5 minutes, stirring frequently.

Switch off the sauté function/transfer the ingredients to your soup maker. Add the potatoes and vegetable stock.

Ensure you do not go over the MAX line of your soup maker. If required, top up with more boiling water to get to the MIN line.

Set the soup maker setting to smooth.

Spinach & Mushroom

Serves 4   Calories: 96 (per serving)

Ingredients

1tbsp olive oil

1 medium onion, chopped

2 cloves garlic, crushed

250g mushrooms, sliced

200g spinach, chopped

800ml vegetable stock

3tbsp crème fraiche

Making It

Heat the olive oil in your soup maker or saucepan.

Add the chopped onion and sauté for 2 to 3 minutes.

Add the crushed garlic and mushrooms. Sauté for a further 5 minutes, stirring frequently.

Transfer the ingredients to your soup maker/switch off the sauté function on your soup maker.

Add the spinach and vegetable stock. Ensure you don't go above the MAX line in your soup maker. If needed, top up to the MIN line with hot water.

Put the lid on and select the smooth setting.

Once finished, add the crème fraiche. Stir in or use the manual blend function.

Cabbage Soup

Serves 4   Calories: 94 (per serving)

Ingredients

1 medium onion, chopped

2 cloves garlic, crushed

500g Savoy cabbage, shredded

1 green pepper, chopped

400g can chopped tomatoes

1 tsp mixed herbs

700ml vegetable stock

Making It

Add all the ingredients to your soup maker.

Ensure you don't go over the MAX line of your soup maker. If you need to, top up with more boiling water to the MIN line.

Set the soup maker to the chunky setting.

Roast Vegetable Soup

Serves 4   Calories: 202 (per serving)

Ingredients

1 to 2tbsp olive oil

2 red peppers, chopped into chunks and deseeded

3 courgettes, halved and cut into chunks

2 medium carrots (approx. 120g), chopped into chunks

2 parsnips (approx.160g), chopped into chunks

1 sweet potato, washed & chopped into chunks

2 medium tomatoes, washed and halved

1 red onion, peeled and chopped into chunks

1 head garlic, outer papery skin removed

2tsp dried mixed herbs

850ml vegetable stock

Making It

Heat the oven to 200°C/gas mark 6.

Lay all the vegetables out on a baking tray (or 2 if they don't fit on 1). Drizzle with the olive oil; toss the vegetables to ensure they are all covered. Sprinkle the dried herbs across the vegetables.

Roast for around 45 minutes or until they are soft and cooked through. Remove from the oven. Squeeze the garlic cloves from their skins. Make sure you don't burn your fingers when squeezing them – you might need a knife to help you cut away some of the skin.

Transfer the roasted vegetables to your soup maker and add the vegetable stock.

Ensure you don't go above the MAX line in your soup maker. If needed, top up to the MIN line with hot water.

Put the lid on and select the smooth setting.

Broccoli & Pesto

Serves 4   Calories: 155 (per serving)

Ingredients

300g broccoli, chopped

1 medium onion, chopped

100g potato, scrubbed and chopped

800ml vegetable stock

3tbsp crème fraiche

1 tbsp. green pesto

Making It

Add the broccoli, onion, potato and stock to your soup maker.

Ensure you don't go above the MAX line in your soup maker. If needed, top up to the MIN line with hot water.

Put the lid on and select the smooth setting.

Stir in the crème fraiche and green pesto. Use the manual blend function for 15 to 20 seconds to combine.

Red Lentil & Garlic

Serves 4   Calories: 115 (per serving)

Ingredients

1tbsp olive oil

1 medium onion, chopped

3 cloves garlic, chopped

200g red lentils, washed

2 medium carrots (approx. 120g), chopped

1tsp mixed dried herbs

850ml vegetable stock

Making It

Heat the olive oil in your soup maker if it has a sauté function. If not, heat in a pan.

Add the chopped onion and sauté for 2 to 3 minutes. Add the garlic and continue to sauté for a further 2 minutes, stirring frequently.

Switch off the sauté function/transfer the ingredients to your soup maker. Add the remaining ingredients and stir to combine.

Ensure you do not go over the MAX line of your soup maker. If required, top up with more boiling water to get to the MIN line.

Set the soup maker setting to smooth.

Red Pepper & Chilli

Serves 4   Calories: 130 (per serving)

Ingredients

1 tbsp. olive oil

1 medium onion, chopped

2 garlic cloves, crushed

2 red peppers (approx. 350g), chopped

1 potato (approx.100g), peeled & chopped

2 fresh red chillies, sliced

750ml cups chicken stock

Making It

Heat the olive oil in your soup maker or saucepan.

Add the chopped onion and sauté for 2 to 3 minutes.

Add the crushed garlic, red pepper and sliced chillies. Sauté for a further 2 to 3 minutes, stirring frequently.

Transfer the ingredients to your soup maker/switch off the sauté function on your soup maker.

Add the chopped potato and chicken stock to your soup maker. Ensure you don't go above the MAX line in your soup maker. If needed, top up to the MIN line with hot water.

Put the lid on and select the smooth setting.

MEAT SOUPS

Coconut Curry Chicken

Serves 4   Calories: 194 (per serving)

Ingredients

300g fresh green beans, trimmed and chopped

250g cooked chicken, shredded

1 medium onion, chopped finely

3 spring onions, chopped

2 garlic cloves, crushed

4 fresh lime leaves

2 tbsp. green curry paste

2 tbsp. fish sauce

600ml chicken stock

350ml coconut milk (light)

Making It

Add all the ingredients to your soup maker and stir well to mix ingredients.

Ensure you don't go above the MAX line in your soup maker. If needed, top up to the MIN line with hot water.

Put the lid on and select the chunky setting.

Discard the lime leaves before serving.

Sweet Potato & Bacon

Serves 4   Calories: 207 (per serving)

Ingredients

1 tbsp. olive oil

1 medium onion, chopped

2 garlic cloves, crushed

520g sweet potatoes (approx.4 potatoes), peeled and chopped

100g bacon lardons

1 tsp. dried basil

1 tsp. ground cumin

2 tsp. smoked paprika

900ml vegetable stock

Making It

Heat the olive oil in your soup maker if it has a sauté function, if not, heat it in a saucepan.

Add the onion, garlic and chopped bacon and sauté for about 4-5 minutes.

Switch off the sauté function on your soup maker/transfer onion and garlic to your soup maker.

Add the remaining ingredients and stir to combine well.

Ensure you don't go above the MAX line in your soup maker. If needed, top up to the MIN line with hot water. Put the lid on and select the smooth setting.

Chicken & Sweetcorn

Serves 4   Calories: 194

Ingredients

1 tbsp. olive oil

1 medium onion, chopped

150g cooked chicken, shredded

300g sweetcorn

150g egg noodles, chopped into small pieces

1 teaspoon ground cinnamon

900ml chicken stock

Making It

Heat the olive oil in your soup maker if it has a sauté function, if not, heat it in a saucepan.

Add the onion and garlic and sauté for about 4-5 minutes.

Switch off the sauté function on your soup maker/transfer onion and garlic to your soup maker.

Add the remaining ingredients to your soup maker.

Ensure you don't go above the MAX line in your soup maker. If needed, top up to the MIN line with hot water.

Put the lid on and select the chunky setting.

Bacon & Lentil

Serves 4   Calories: 186 (per serving)

Ingredients

1tbsp olive oil

200g split red lentils, rinsed

1 potato (approx.100g), scrubbed and chopped finely

1 small carrot (approx. 50g), peeled and chopped finely

1 medium onion, chopped

1000ml chicken stock

4 rashers bacon, fat removed, chopped

Making It

Heat the oil in your soup maker if it has a sauté function. Alternatively heat the oil in saucepan.

Add the onions and chopped bacon and sauté for 2 to 3 minutes.

Switch off the sauté function/transfer the onions and bacon to your soup maker.

Add the remaining ingredients.

Ensure you don't go above the MAX line in your soup maker. If required, top up to the MIN line with hot water.

Put the lid on and select the chunky setting.

Thai Red Chicken

Serves 4   Calories: 147 (per serving)

Ingredients

2 chicken breasts cooked (approx. 290g), diced

3 tbsp. Thai Red curry paste

1 lime (juice)

1 lemongrass stalk (dried), chopped

1 red chilli sliced (deseed if you prefer a milder taste)

2 garlic cloves, crushed

2 tbsp. fresh root ginger Grated

4 spring onions, sliced

1 litre chicken stock

Making It

Add all the ingredients to your soup maker.

Ensure you don't go above the MAX line in your soup maker. If needed, top up to the MIN line with hot water.

Put the lid on and select the smooth setting.

Garlic Lemon Chicken

Serves 4   Calories: 227 (per serving)

Ingredients

250g cooked chicken, shredded

200g potatoes, peeled and cubed

70g carrot, peeled and chopped

3 cloves garlic, crushed

Zest and juice from 1 lemon

100g egg noodles

1 tbsp. flour

1 litre chicken stock

Making It

Add all ingredients in your soup maker, breaking the noodles up into small pieces as you put them in. Stir to combine well.

Ensure you don't go above the MAX line in your soup maker. If needed, top up to the MIN line with hot water.

Put the lid on and select the chunky setting.

Bolognese Beef Soup

Serves 4   Calories: 147 (per serving)

Ingredients

1tbsp olive oil

200g beef mince, cooked

1 onion, chopped

3 cloves garlic, crushed

2tsp mixed dried herbs

400g can chopped tomatoes

750ml beef stock

50g grated parmesan (optional)

Making It

Add all the ingredients to your soup maker apart from the parmesan.

Ensure you don't go over the MAX line on your soup maker. If required, top up to the MIN line with hot water.

Set the soup maker to the smooth setting.

Once finished, stir in the parmesan cheese until melted (optional).

Chicken & Tarragon

Serves 4   Calories: 171 (per serving)

Ingredients

1 tbsp. olive oil

1 medium onion, chopped finely

3 celery stalks (approx.120g.), chopped

2 medium carrots (approx.240g), peeled and chopped

2 garlic cloves, crushed

250g cooked chicken, shredded

1tbsp fresh tarragon, chopped, or 1tsp dried tarragon

850ml chicken stock

Making It

Heat the oil in your soup maker if it has a sauté function. Alternatively heat the oil in a saucepan.

Add the chopped onions and sauté for 5 minutes. Add the garlic, celery and carrots and sauté for a further 2 to 3 minutes, stirring frequently.

Switch off the sauté function on your soup maker/transfer ingredients to your soup maker.

Add the remaining ingredients. Ensure you are between the MIN and MAX lines on your soup maker. Add more hot water if required.

Set on chunky setting.

Chicken & Mushroom

Serves 4   Calories: 212 (per serving)

Ingredients

200g cooked chicken, shredded

100g mushrooms, sliced

150g small pasta shells/shapes

1tsp mixed dried herbs

1L chicken stock

Making It

Add all ingredients to your soup maker. Stir to combine well.

Ensure you don't go above the MAX line in your soup maker. If needed, top up to the MIN line with hot water.

Put the lid on and select the chunky setting.

Creamy Chicken Soup

Ingredients

200g cooked chicken, shredded

2 cloves garlic, crushed

1 medium onion, chopped

200g potatoes, scrubbed and diced

1litre chicken stock

2tbsp crème fraiche

Making It

Add all the ingredients, except the crème fraiche, to your soup maker and stir to combine.

Ensure you don't go above the MAX line in your soup maker. If needed, top up to the MIN line with hot water.

Put the lid on and select the smooth setting.

Stir in the crème fraiche and manually blend for 15 to 20 seconds.

Want to make it less creamy?

Just leave out the cream and potatoes (you might need to increase the stock volume).

Thai Green Curry

Serves 4   Calories: 188 (per serving)

Ingredients

200g cooked chicken, shredded

2tbsp Thai Green Curry Paste

400ml coconut milk

1tbsp light brown sugar

½ tsp Thai fish sauce

Juice of 1 lime

8 baby sweetcorn, halved

100g mangetout

750ml chicken stock

Fresh basil, chopped (optional for garnish)

Making It

Add all the ingredients to your soup maker and stir to combine.

Ensure you don't go above the MAX line in your soup maker. If needed, top up to the MIN line with hot water.

Put the lid on and select the smooth setting.

Garnish with fresh basil (optional)

Leftover Turkey Soup

Serves 4   Calories: 140 (per serving)

Ingredients

1tbsp olive oil

200g (approx.) turkey meat, shredded

2 small carrots, sliced

1 leek, chopped

1 red onion, chopped

2 cloves garlic, crushed

1tsp each dried thyme, dried sage

850ml turkey or chicken stock

Making It

Heat the oil in your soup maker if it has a sauté function. Alternatively heat the oil in a saucepan.

Add the chopped onions, garlic, leek and carrot. Sauté for 5 minutes, stirring frequently.

Switch off the sauté function on your soup maker/transfer the ingredients to your soup maker.

Add the remaining ingredients to your soup maker.

Ensure you don't go above the MAX line in your soup maker. If needed, top up to the MIN line with hot water.

Put the lid on and select the chunky setting.

Gammon & Brussel Sprout

Serves 4   Calories: 209 (per serving)

Ingredients

1tbsp olive oil

1 medium onion, finely sliced

2 cloves garlic, crushed

1 parsnip, finely sliced

1 carrot, finely sliced

250g Brussel sprouts, finely sliced

300g cooked gammon, shredded

800ml vegetable stock

Making It

Heat the oil in your soup maker if it has a sauté function. Alternatively heat the oil in a saucepan.

Add the chopped onions, garlic, parsnips, carrots and Brussel sprouts. Sauté for 8-10 minutes, stirring frequently.

Switch off the sauté function on your soup maker/transfer the ingredients to your soup maker.

Add the remaining ingredients to your soup maker.

Ensure you don't go above the MAX line in your soup maker. If needed, top up to the MIN line with hot water.

Put the lid on and select the chunky setting.

Spicy Turkey

Ingredients

250g cooked turkey, shredded

1 medium onion, chopped

3 cloves garlic, crushed

1 medium potato, scrubbed and chopped

1 tin 400g chopped tomatoes

2 red chillies, finely sliced

1tsp ground cumin

850ml chicken or turkey stock

Making It

Heat the oil in your soup maker if it has a sauté function. Alternatively heat the oil in a saucepan.

Add the chopped onions and garlic. Sauté for 5 minutes, stirring frequently.

Switch off the sauté function on your soup maker/transfer the ingredients to your soup maker.

Add the remaining ingredients to your soup maker.

Ensure you don't go above the MAX line in your soup maker. If needed, top up to the MIN line with hot water.

Put the lid on and select the smooth setting.

Ham & Pineapple

Serves 4   Calories: 225 (per serving)

Ingredients

1tbsp olive oil

250g cooked ham, chopped

200g pineapple chunks

1 medium onion, chopped

1 clove garlic, crushed

2 sticks celery, sliced

1 medium potato, peeled and diced

850ml vegetable stock

Making It

Heat the oil in your soup maker if it has a sauté function. Alternatively heat the oil in a saucepan.

Add the chopped onions, garlic and celery. Sauté for 5 minutes, stirring frequently.

Switch off the sauté function on your soup maker/transfer the ingredients to your soup maker.

Add the remaining ingredients to your soup maker.

Ensure you don't go above the MAX line in your soup maker. If needed, top up to the MIN line with hot water.

Put the lid on and select the chunky setting.

Split Pea & Ham

Serves 4   Calories: 135 (per serving)

Ingredients

1 tbsp. olive oil

1 medium onion

2 cloves garlic, crushed

300g green split peas, rinsed

200g quality cooked ham, shredded

850ml vegetable stock

Making It

Heat the oil in your soup maker if it has a sauté function. Alternatively heat the oil in a saucepan.

Add the chopped onions and garlic. Sauté for 5 minutes, stirring frequently.

Switch off the sauté function on your soup maker/transfer the ingredients to your soup maker.

Add the remaining ingredients to your soup maker.

Ensure you don't go above the MAX line in your soup maker. If needed, top up to the MIN line with hot water.

Put the lid on and select the smooth setting.

Minestrone

Ingredients

1tbsp olive oil

100g bacon lardons

1 medium onion, chopped

2 cloves garlic, crushed

2 medium carrots, peeled and sliced

150g green beans, trimmed and sliced in half

3tbsp tomato puree

400g tinned tomatoes

100g small pasta shells

400g can kidney beans, drained

750ml vegetable stock

Making It

Heat the oil in your soup maker if it has a sauté function. Alternatively heat the oil in a saucepan.

Add the bacon lardons and stir to coat in the oil. Allow to cook for 8 minutes or until crispy and brown. Add the onion and garlic and sauté for a further 2 to 3 minutes.

Switch off the sauté function on your soup maker/transfer the ingredients to your soup maker.

Add the remaining ingredients to your soup maker.

Ensure you don't go above the MAX line in your soup maker. If needed, top up to the MIN line with hot water.

Put the lid on and select the chunky setting.

Seriously Garlicky Chicken

Serves 4   Calories: 286 (per serving)

Ingredients

2tbsp olive oil

1 medium onion, sliced

2 cooked chicken breasts

35 cloves garlic, roasted

5 cloves garlic, crushed

1 medium potato, scrubbed and diced

Juice of half a lime

1 red chilli, sliced (deseeded if you prefer)

750ml vegetable stock

Making It

The clue is of course in the name – but this soup isn't for everyone. You must have a love, bordering on obsession with garlic to really enjoy this one.

Preheat the oven to 190°C/Gas Mark 5. Slice the very tips off the 35 cloves of garlic, but leave their skins on. Place on a baking tray and drizzle with the olive oil. Shake to make sure each one is coated. Cover the garlic cloves with foil. Roast in the oven for around 35 to 40 minutes. Check they are golden and soft. Set aside to cool.

Once the garlic cloves are cool enough to touch, gently squeeze each one to remove the skin.

Add the 35 roasted garlic cloves, together with the remaining ingredients in your soup maker.

Ensure you don't go above the MAX line in your soup maker. If needed, top up to the MIN line with hot water.

Select the smooth setting on your soup maker.

Chicken & Asparagus

Serves 4   Calories: 215 (per serving)

Ingredients

1tbsp olive oil

150g cooked chicken breast, diced

400g asparagus, chopped

1 medium onion, chopped

1 garlic clove, crushed

1 medium potato, scrubbed and chopped

2tbsp crème fraiche

750ml chicken stock

Making It

Heat the oil in your soup maker if it has a sauté function. Alternatively heat the oil in a saucepan.

Add the onion and garlic. Sauté for about 5 minutes.

Switch off the sauté function on your soup maker/transfer the ingredients to your soup maker.

Add the remaining ingredients to your soup maker, except the crème fraiche.

Ensure you don't go above the MAX line in your soup maker. If needed, top up to the MIN line with hot water.

Put the lid on and select the chunky setting.

When finished, stir in the crème fraiche and use the manual blend setting for 15 to 20 seconds.

Beef & Onion

Serves 4   Calories: 197 (per serving)

Ingredients

1tbsp olive oil

300g diced beef, cooked and cubed

3 medium onions, chopped

1 potato (approx. 100g) scrubbed and chopped

1 stick celery, chopped

800ml beef/vegetable stock

Making It

Heat the oil in your soup maker if it has a sauté function. Alternatively heat the oil in a saucepan.

Add the onions and sauté for about 5 minutes.

Switch off the sauté function on your soup maker/transfer the ingredients to your soup maker.

Add all the remaining ingredients to your soup maker. Stir the ingredients.

Ensure you don't go above the MAX line in your soup maker. If needed, top up to the MIN line with hot water.

Put the lid on and select the chunky setting.

Mulligatawny Soup

Serves 4   Calories: 202 (per serving)

Ingredients

1tbsp olive oil

150g cooked chicken, shredded

1 medium onion, chopped

2 cloves garlic, crushed

2tsp tomato puree

4 fresh tomatoes, chopped

1 inch fresh root ginger, grated

1 medium carrot (approx. 60g), chopped

1 Bramley apple, peeled, cored and chopped

1tsp curry powder

750ml chicken stock

150ml single cream

Making It

Heat the oil in your soup maker if it has a sauté function. Alternatively heat the oil in a saucepan.

Add the onions and sauté for about 2 minutes. Add the ginger and garlic and sauté for a further 2-3 minutes.

Switch off the sauté function on your soup maker/transfer the ingredients to your soup maker.

Add all the remaining ingredients to your soup maker, except the single cream. Stir the ingredients.

Ensure you don't go above the MAX line in your soup maker. If needed, top up to the MIN line with hot water.

Put the lid on and select the smooth setting.

Once finished, add the single cream and stir in.

FISH SOUPS

Salmon & Dill

Serves 4   Calories: 277 (per serving)

Ingredients

1tbsp olive oil

1 onion, chopped

400g can of chopped tomatoes

418g can of boneless red salmon, drained and flaked

1tbsp fresh lemon juice

2tbsps fresh dill, chopped

150ml single cream

850ml fish stock

Making It

Heat the olive oil in your soup maker or saucepan.

Add the chopped onion and sauté for 2 to 3 minutes.

Transfer the ingredients to your soup maker/switch off the sauté function on your soup maker.

Add the remaining ingredients, except the chopped dill and single cream. Ensure you don't go above the MAX line in your soup maker. If needed, top up to the MIN line with hot water.

Put the lid on and select the smooth setting.

When the soup has finished add the chopped dill and the single cream. Stir in.

Curried Haddock

Serves 4   Calories: 227 (per serving)

Ingredients

400g haddock fillet, skinless and boneless, cut into chunks

1 medium onion, chopped

2 garlic cloves, crushed

1 inch piece of ginger, peeled and grated/finely chopped

1 red chilli, sliced (deseeded if you prefer a milder taste)

1 medium potato, scrubbed and chopped

1tsp each ground cumin, garam masala, mild chilli powder

2tbsp tomato puree

800ml fish stock

Making It

Add all the ingredients to your soup maker.

Ensure you don't go above the MAX line in your soup maker. If needed, top up to the MIN line with hot water.

Put the lid on and select the smooth setting.

Thai Fish Curry

Ingredients

400g cod, skinless and boneless, cut into chunks

1 inch fresh ginger, peeled and grated (or ½ tsp ground ginger)

1 red chilli, finely sliced (deseed if you prefer a milder taste)

2tbsp Thai green curry paste

1tbsp Thai fish sauce

2 Kaffir lime leaves

Juice of half a lime

400ml coconut milk (light)

350ml vegetable stock

Coriander leaves (optional for garnish)

Making It

Add all the ingredients, except the coriander, to your soup maker.

Ensure you don't go over the MAX line of your soup maker. If you need to, top up to the MIN line with hot boiling water, or more coconut milk.

Set to the chunky setting on your soup maker.

Once complete, garnish with coriander (optional).

Easy Prawn Soup

Serves 4   Calories: 134 (per serving)

Ingredients

225g peeled tiger prawns

2 ripe tomatoes, chopped

1 red onion, chopped

1 clove garlic, crushed

1tbsp tomato puree

1tsp dried mixed herbs

850ml fish or vegetable stock

3tbsp crème fraiche

Making It

Add all the ingredients to your soup maker, apart from the crème fraiche.

Ensure you don't go above the MAX line in your soup maker. If needed, top up to the MIN line with hot water.

Set the soup maker off on the smooth setting.

When finished, add the crème fraiche and stir or manually blend.

Cod, Sweet Potato & Parsley

Serves 4   Calories: 151 (per serving)

Ingredients

1 medium onion, chopped

60g carrot, chopped

200g cod

150g sweet potato

40g parsley, chopped

3tbsp crème fraiche

800ml fish or vegetable stock

Making It

Add all the ingredients to the soup maker, except the crème fraiche and parsley.

Ensure you don't go over the MAX line of your soup maker. Top up with boiling water if you are not at the MIN line.

Set on the smooth setting.

Once complete, add the chopped parsley (reserving a little for garnish if required) and crème fraiche. Stir in or manually blend.

HOMEMADE STOCK

Quick Tips

- It is important to try and cool down homemade stock as soon as possible and storing it in the fridge or freezer as soon as you can. You can speed up the time it takes to cool down by putting the saucepan or pot in a sink of cold water.

- Stock can be stored in the fridge for up to 3 days or the freezer for up to 3 months. Store in suitable containers, labelling them with the date and what it is (I would most definitely forget otherwise!)

- Store meat bones in the freezer until you have enough to make a stock.

- Store stock in useful measured out volumes, such as 750ml – that way when you are ready to make a soup you can take one out and just top up with some more water if required.

- You can spice up stocks by adding in chillies, ginger and other spices.

Vegetable Stock

You can use whatever vegetables you have in the kitchen. The following is merely a guide and can be adapted according to your tastes and what you have available. Adding some herbs will boost the taste – just choose your favourite ones.

Ingredients

4 pints of cold water

2 celery stalks, chopped

2 leeks, chopped

1 inch fresh ginger, chopped

5 carrots, chopped

2 bay leaves

3 garlic cloves, chopped

1 onion, chopped

1 tsp mixed herbs (or any herbs of your choice)

Making It

Add all the ingredients to a large pot and bring to the boil. Turn down the heat and leave to simmer for around 60 minutes. Check on it periodically to skim off any scum that has risen to the surface.

If you want to reduce the volume (which also enhances the flavour), allow some air to get into the pot by placing the lid on at an angle.

Use a fine sieve to strain the stock. Discard the vegetables. Try the stock to see what it tastes like. If you prefer a stronger taste you can simmer again, with the lid off.

Don't season the stock now; wait until you are ready to use it.

If you are not ready to use the stock immediately store it in the fridge or in the freezer.

Beef Stock

Save any beef bones from Sunday Roasts or other meals. You can store them in the freezer until you have enough to make a stock from them.

Ingredients

1.3kg beef bones (from cooked joints)

2 onions, cut into quarters

2 celery sticks, chopped

2 carrots, chopped

1 bay leaf

1tsp dried thyme (or other dried herbs)

10 black peppercorns, lightly crushed

4 pints of cold water.

Making It

Preheat the oven to 230C/Gas Mark 8.

Place the bones into a large roasting tin. Roast for around 30 minutes until the bones have darkened.

Add the onions, carrots and celery and baste with the fat from the roasting tin. Roast for a further 20 minutes, or until the vegetables are soft.

Transfer the bones and vegetables to a large saucepan and add the herbs and water. Bring to the boil and then reduce to a simmer. Leave to simmer for 2 to 3 hours, periodically skimming any scum off the surface.

Using a fine sieve, strain the mix and taste. If you want a stronger taste simmer again to reduce the stock.

If you are not using it immediately, store in the fridge or freezer (once fully cooled). Any fat that rises to the top can be removed.

Chicken Stock

Chicken stock really intensifies the flavour of a soup. If you regularly have a chicken roast making this stock up shouldn't be hard.

Ingredients

1 large chicken carcass (or 2 small ones)

2 onions, quartered

2 celery sticks, chopped

2 carrots, chopped

1 garlic clove, chopped

1 bay leaf

Sprig of thyme

10 black peppercorns, lightly crushed

3 pints cold water

Making It

You will probably need to break the carcass up to fit it in your pot. Add all the ingredients to a large pot and bring to the boil. Once boiled, turn down the heat and leave to simmer for 2 to 3 hours. Check on it periodically to skim away any scum that has risen to the surface.

Use a fine sieve to strain the liquid. Check the taste and simmer again to reduce it further if required.

If you are not using the stock immediately cool it down and then store it in the fridge or freezer.

Fish Stock

Fish stock is easy enough to make and is much quicker than the other stocks. If you don't have your own fish bones to use ask your local fishmonger if they can spare any.

Ingredients

1kg fish bones and trimmings (from white fish)

1 onion, chopped

1 celery stick, chopped

2 carrots, sliced

3 garlic cloves, chopped

1 bay leaf

8 black peppercorns, crushed

200ml white wine

4 pints of cold water

Making It

Make sure the fish bones and any other trimmings you are using are rinsed thoroughly. Add everything to a large pot. Bring to the boil and then reduce to a simmer. Simmer on a low heat for about 20 minutes. Check periodically and skim any scum from the surface.

Using a fine sieve, strain the mixture. Discard the bones and any other trimmings. If you want to reduce the stock further (and intensify the flavour) simmer it with the lid off for a bit longer.

Croutons

Croutons make a lovely addition to a soup. You can buy premade ones, or if you have time, make some of your own.

Ingredients

French bread/ciabatta/sliced bread (crusts removed), cut into small cubes

Extra virgin olive oil/sunflower oil or a groundnut oil

Making It

Preheated the oven (200C/Gas Mark 6).

Place the bread cubes on a baking tray and brush with oil.

Allow to bake for 10 to 15 minutes or until they are crisp.

They can be stored in an airtight container for up to a week.

Tip: Make garlic croutons by gently sautéing 3 cloves of crushed garlic in a little olive oil, for just 20 to 30 seconds. Add the bread cubes and fry on a gentle heat for a further 2 or 3 minutes until crisp. Make sure you turn them over in the pan so they are coated by the oil.

Thanks for Reading & Free Books

Dear Reader,

I really hope that you have enjoyed the recipes in this book.

If you have found this book useful I would **really** appreciate it if you could spare a moment please to leave a review on Amazon.

It really inspires and encourages me to keep on creating books. If you have any suggestions or questions please do feel free to get in contact with me at liana@lianaskitchen.co.uk

If you have any soup recipe suggestions, I would love to hear from you too!

Whenever I publish a new book on Kindle I always give it away for free (only for a few days!) If you want to find out when a new book is released, you can sign up to my VIP list right here;

www.lianaskitchen.co.uk/VIP

Enjoy your soup!

Liana x

OTHER TITLES

Are you interested in reading any other books by Liana Green?

The #1 bestselling **Nutri Ninja Recipe Book – 70 Smoothie Recipes for Weight Loss, Increased Energy and Improved Health** is available from Amazon UK, USA and other Amazon stores worldwide, as well as the other books in the same series.

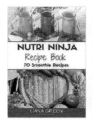   

INDEX

15837242R10079

Printed in Great Britain
by Amazon